To JEFF
You ARE AWESOME!
. ENJOY
ORANGE!!!

ORANGE

ORANGE

A slice for you
A slice for me
There are enough slices to go around.

HUMAN

I am human
I breathe

I love
I lust

I laugh
I loathe

I lounge
I long

I look
I lurch

MORE

More flavors
More desires

More colors
More designers

That one has vigilant eyes
The one who sits in the corner of the diner
With a newspaper,
Every paper
That gets flipped through leaves its residue.
New knowledge.

I water me

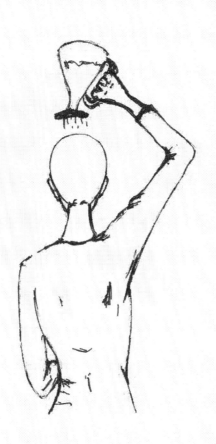

In communion with nature, faith and fantasies

I plant a sun garden with orange and yellow flowers.

A moon garden with black, white and blue flowers

In my heart.

To bloom beautifully day and night.

Lessons for lasting insight.

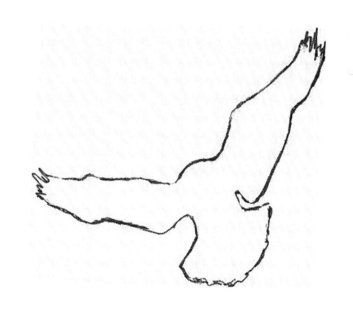

A COLORFUL CAST OF CHARACTERS

I am oil,
water,
sweet,
tart,
The complexity and full flavor of a
chocolate truffle,
The seemingly demure surface of
a cherry cordial hiding a sweet center,
Rapunzel in the tower,
Cinderella at the palace ball.

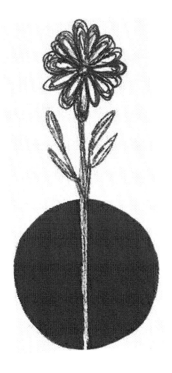

THE ART OF HOSTING

You have to serve the best wine
From your vineyard
At every function
She said,
Add sweeteners, extra yeasts and fining agents to your finest grapes
To achieve the desired flavor and lucidity.
It is like adding life to years
And adding years to life.

THE MUSE

The Painter
The Masterpiece

Like sunset tucking into the horizon in anticipation of the moon,
You lay down a foundation for growth,
Deep roots, solid trunk.

In anticipation of your desires,
A dream that shimmers in the distance.
You mold the you that helps fortify your dreams.

PLAY OF LIGHT

What is a gloomy day?

Try teal

    It would heighten your zeal.

Rock classic red

    Like you have a crown on your head.

Think pink

    It is the sweetest ink.

Yell yellow

    Don't be mellow.

Shock in electric blue

    All seasons hot hue.

Go for gold

    It never gets old.

GINGER

Soul lifter,
The battery that powers your light always
Not just on dark days.

Soul lifter,
One that seasons you
With spices for days.

Soul lifter,
The sun
That longs to nourish you,
To enrich your power banks.

Soul lifter,
The one who pours
premium rocket fuel into your tanks.

Keep them close.

You are here

You are worthy.

CRYSTAL

Good vibrations are like

The smell of brand new Italian leather shoes,

The sweet smell of a gift package from London,

The sheen of silk,

The allure of the Grand Canal in Venice.

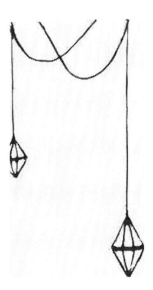

FLOURISH

A wonder among flowers,

Stay in lustful focus

As the sun colors flowers

That you be doused in diamonds and dramatic ballads

That you witness all things flourish and dance in endless variations

That you radiate light

With every swerve.

ORGANIC

Your mind is an elixir
You can make magic.

Do not let your fears eclipse your sun.

MENU

Waiter : Have you decided what to order yet?

Me   : I feel like every part of me;
          Brain, heart, soul, gut
          Is on its own train track,
          Railcars of pleated thoughts,
          Battles looming on multiple war fronts within like
          ⊠Do I want lentil soup or black bean soup⊠

SWEET STRINGS OF LIGHT

I missed your call and all of a sudden
The harbour is still
The sea is blue
The trees are greener
The sun is brighter
Sand is yellow and dry
The moon is wild
Stars are twinkly
I feel alive again

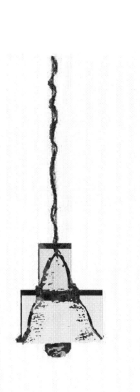

Like the broken pottery molded back with gold lacquer,
She places pieces of her broken spirit
Carefully together,
Molds it with all the colors of her dreams
Because she knows her resolute spirit
can still lead her to the moon.

DESERT FLOWER

I yearn for the type of silence
That elicits sound reflections.

Silence that magnifies
Fragrant memories of vanished flowers.

A story that belongs to a different time?

Where a stranger's intended good deed is not questioned.

Where we serve tea and offer a bed to strangers on a cold night;
before they set out on their journey the next morning.

Where all the children can play at the village square;
listen to folktales narrated by elders,

Sing the moon song joyfully as they go to fetch water
from the stream at sunset with no fear of danger.

LEMON

On your quest,
Should your journey be threatened by a cloudburst,

    Take refuge in a nearby town,
Learn a new culture,
Learn new skills with wild attentive eyes,
Lend your ears to foreign tricks.
Proceed on your journey
With new eyes in a whole new light.

SIT REGAL AT THE WHEEL

You find the light easily

when you are at the wheel.

You are never alone,
The sun will keep you warm in that cold thought
And help color your flowers.
The moon and stars will illuminate your path
And help settle your disturbed emotions.

?

What makes your magic come alive?
A sunbeam into your life.

What paints your heart
Like mosaic art?

We get lost sometimes

We loose a few dimes

We make mistakes

We pull up stakes

We learn.

SKIN

Swimming in a sea of broken glass in search of diamonds,
Magnetically drawn to false vibrations
Ornamented in false glitter
Like fruit flies to sugar,
It is time to take off the metals.

FRUIT FARM CON

Persimmons and Tangerines grow here,
Please pick sagely.

DO NOT TANGO WITH ME

You wore a sequin suit
You sang a dreadful tune.

MAHOGANY

You open up the house in your heart to a guest

The guest walks in and decks the halls with
        priceless diamonds
Fills up your shelf with the best books
        Bakes you the Cadillac of all carrot cakes
Plants the most beautiful flowers in your garden
        Carving an indelible imprint in your heart.

MYSTERY BOX ON MY DOOR STEP

You knocked on my door bearing a bouquet of thorns,
I could hear the sirens,
I could see the yellow tape,
I could hear the news already
But I still let you in.

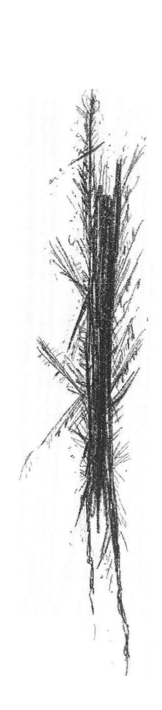

Surround yourself with a sea of light.

Like trees planted by streams of water

You will yield fruits in your season.

-Genesis.

A GREAT SLICE OF LIFE

In a moment of silent reflection
I realize how wonderful it is

To whisper into the silent sea,
To hear nature's symphony,
To disappear into a new world,
To fetch from the deep wells of clarity,
To breathe in heavenly air on earth.

Virtual Reality.

ROUND ABOUT

Walking through Orange grove
for the first time on a warm afternoon in Sandton.
I was overcome with nostalgic feelings,
I began to wonder,
'Have I lived here before in a preceding lifetime,
drank this air,
walked this street,
Are we all just walking around in circles?

THE FLAME THAT BECAME A BONFIRE

The Bristlecone pine grew from a seedling.
Keep the light in your eyes,
That little spark
Can light up a whole city.
For as you doubt, so must you believe.

DEUX EX MACHINA

Fear
Insinuated itself inward
With disturbing ease
Like a horror in a dream.

Fear creeped in and I set up a room for it
In the squares of my mind,
I set fire to keep it warm on cold nights,
Served it hot tea in the morning,
Made it my blanket and confidant,
Until I noticed a silver tint
in the gray cloud of doubt on my ceiling.

THE FLEETING CLOUDINESS OF A FLAWED MIND

I have shipped jars of poisoned rose petals
to an old abandoned Brooklyn apartment.
Built walls and burnt bridges.
I made darkness my mirror.
Set fire to vintage Hermes
So as not to lend Sade.

Some mornings
I wake up in a cold sweat,
Feeling a mayhem of emotions
Like an oil lamp floating on water
No shores to arrive.

Alarmed by things that could happen,
Might happen,
Might not happen.
Panic sets in
Before I even set out.

The night is gone
But it's dream still lingers;
In a slow film of a thunder shower
A strange monstrous creature
In grim velvety gray color of dread
Stands beside my favorite chair in a deserted castle
Just staring directly at me
Lightning strikes, accentuating
It's motionless image and unblinking daemon eyes I can't move
I am trapped
Terror running through my veins
Muttering voiceless screams
My eyelids too heavy to blink...

Run from naysayers,
Feel the wind of change.

Pay attention to the traffic signals within.

PRICE POINT

In a busy market place that sat on a land
of undiscovered rare gem stones,
A coal seller's child playing hide and seek in the market
found a stone and kept it as a toy.
His father took it from him
and presented it to the Village Chief.
The Village Chief summoned his merchant from the city,
The merchant arrived,
saw the stone,
called the Chief aside
and told him they were about to be rich.

In search for more rare stones,
The market vendors were evacuated
And robbed of their means of livelihood.
The family who discovered the stone was given
Enough cowries to last them for a week.
The Chief married a new wife
and christened a new Peugeot 504.
The merchant opens a Swiss bank account.

HOT HOUSE

Not going to set myself on fire to keep you warm again,
I am half burnt
and you are striking the rocks again!

Sometimes,
I think about other people's lives;
Their secret wishes and hidden hopes,
Moments of happiness or emptiness,
The demands that accompany the twilight of life.

Sometimes,
I think about the fragility of life;
How man-made bullets could pierce through a heart.
How words spoken by man could break hearts, Build walls,
Change the course of human life.

The unnerving reminder that one can be
The prosecutor
The jury
The judge
On other people's lives.

I also think about
How one can awaken another with words,
Elevate another with good deeds,
Soothe another's heart with kindness.

In these moments,
I realize
The magnitude of the power we have
On ourselves
And most importantly on others.
What do you do with your power?

CROWNING GLORY

On a quiet Saturday afternoon
While going through old family photographs
I was trying so hard to remember my Grandmother's voice
A voice that raised me;
Recited my praise poetry,
Sang 'Que Sera Sera' to me at bedtime
While she kept vigil with kerosene lamps and mosquito coils.

I could not remember her voice
But I remembered her compassionate soul,
Her giving heart,
Her loving spirit; that makes the heaven rejoice
And all the great lessons of love learnt from her actions towards
others.
Amama.

IT REALLY TAKES A VILLAGE - Unity Is Strength

When the cry of a newborn is heard,
The entire village erupts in celebration,
Breaking out in joyful songs,
The villagers bring out their best yams and palm wine,
The elders come out to give praises and say prayers bearing

Honey and Sugar to declare
that the child's life be sweet as honey, Salt;
so the child would be a source of joy to the family,
Water;
for a peaceful long life as water has no enemy,
Alligator Pepper;
for the child's lineage to multiply
like the seeds of an alligator pepper,
Bitter kola;
for the child to live a healthy long life,
Kola-nut;
to purge ill fate

For the joy of one
Is the joy of all.

FRUIT BASKET

1. Violence or grace
   Which takes the cake
   Which takes the chair
   The toxic power of rage
   The magic of grace.

2. Love is light
   Hate is heavy.

SWEET DREAMS

The stuff dreams are made of;

Blue evenings,

A beautiful mix of a wild heart,

A warm spirit

And a sweet passionate soul

That Bees hover over.

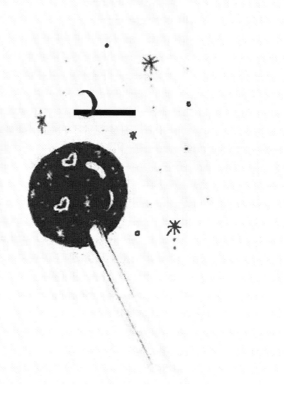

THE SLASH GENERATION

Being made up of so many colors is a blessing,
The dilemma sometimes lies in mixing all these colors
to paint a perfect picture,
A tour de force.

Life is a sea surf of episodes:
The memories
The music
The books
The custom
The lucky choices
The search engine
The color orange
The free rides
The humour
The melodrama
The friendships
The messiness
The confusion
The power of perception
The abstract dreams
The colorful dreams
The dainty smiles
The emotional complexities
The cynicism
The energy
The colorful skies
The fantasies
The gratification
The conquest.

ORANGE JUICE

Do not filter the pulp,
Drink it all in a gulp.
Dry up the seeds
For planting,
Repel flies with the peels for trespassing.

Made in the USA
Middletown, DE
20 June 2018